Investigating Rocks

The Rock Cycle

Will Hurd

Heinemann Library
Chicago, Illinois

Customer Service 888-454-2279
Visit our website at www.heinemannraintree.com

Editorial: Louise Galpine and Rachel Howells
Design: Richard Parker and Tinstar Design Ltd
Original illustrations © Capstone Global Library Ltd
Illustrations: Oxford Designers and Illustrators and David Woodroffe (pages 12 and 18)
Picture research: Hannah Taylor and Fiona Orbell
Production: Alison Parsons

Originated by Dot Gradations Ltd.
Printed and bound in China by Leo Paper Products Ltd.

13 12 11 10 09
10 9 8 7 6 5 4 3 2 1

Library of Congress Cataloging-in-Publication Data
Hurd, Will.
  Investigating rocks : the rock cycle / Will Hurd. -- 1st ed.
    p. cm. -- (Do it yourself)
  Includes bibliographical references and index.
  ISBN 978-1-4329-2308-2 (hc) -- ISBN 978-1-4329-2315-0 (pb)
  1. Petrology. 2. Geochemical cycles. I. Title.
  QE431.2.H86 2008
  552.0078--dc22
                    2008034934

Acknowledgments
The author and publishers are grateful to the following for permission to reproduce copyright material:
© Corbis pp. **15** (Bill Ross), **20** (Gary Braasch), **31** (Louie Psihoyos), **39** (Arno Balzarini/epa), **40** (Phil Schermeister), **41**, **43** (Skyscan); © Dorling Kindersley, Courtesy of the Natural History Museum, London p. **23** (Colin Keates); © Hugo Sonia p. **35**; © istock p. **5** (William Blacke); © PhotoDisc p. **7**; © Photolibrary pp. **4** (Carson Ganci), **13** (Jess Alford), **17** (Olivier Grunewald), **25** (Jacob Halaska), **33** (Image Source), **36** (James Hardy), **37**, **42** (Joel Seth); © Science Photo Library p. **30** (Ted Clutter); © Still Pictures pp. **10** (Biosphoto/BIOS; Bios – Auteurs (droits geres); Bringard Denis), **11** (John Cancalesi); © The Trustees of the British Museum p. **29**.

Cover photograph of red granite rocks on coast, reproduced with permission of © Frank Krahmer (Photolibrary).

The publishers would like to thank Harold Pratt for his invaluable assistance in the preparation of this book.

Every effort has been made to contact copyright holders of any material reproduced in this book. Any omissions will be rectified in subsequent printings if notice is given to the publishers.

Contents

Any words appearing in the text in bold, **like this**, are explained in the glossary.

What Is a Rock?

When you look at a loaf of bread, it is hard to see what it is made up of. You just see the end product—bread. Do a little investigating, though, and you will find that bread is made from several ingredients. The basic building blocks of bread are flour, yeast, sugar, salt, and water. Further investigation shows that these building blocks have building blocks of their own. For example, water is made up of hydrogen and oxygen, and salt is a mixture of sodium and chlorine. Hydrogen, oxygen, sodium, and chlorine are all **elements**. A single piece, or particle, of an element is called an **atom**. Elements are the most basic building blocks of what is called **matter**—bread, wood, and everything else we see, including **rocks**.

Most things are not pure elements, but are **compounds**. A compound is a combination of two or more different elements that are held together and make up a new substance. Water and salt are both compounds. A **mineral** is a type of compound that usually forms as a result of heat and pressure deep within the Earth. (But some minerals can form in water, as you will see in the first experiment.) A rock is a group of minerals that are joined together.

Rocks and everything else on Earth is made up of matter.

Three kinds of rock

There are three different kinds of rocks: igneous, metamorphic, and sedimentary. Each kind of rock forms in a different way.

Igneous rock forms when **magma** cools and hardens. Some igneous rock forms when magma is pushed to the Earth's surface. Igneous rock can also form from magma that never reaches the surface, cooling and hardening underground.

Metamorphic rock forms when old rocks are heated or squeezed to the point that they change into new, different rocks. This only happens beneath the surface of the Earth, where temperatures can get very high and the pressure is great.

Sedimentary rock forms when **sediment** settles into layers in certain places. After that, the sediments become rocks in one of a few different ways.

All rocks change, move, and change again in a long continuous process called the **rock cycle.**

Mount Rushmore in South Dakota is carved from granite, an igneous rock.

About the experiments

Carrying out the experiments in this book will help you to investigate rocks. The experiments use simple everyday materials and tools. Always read through the instructions before you start, and take your time. You will need an adult to help with some of the experiments.

The Rock Cycle

When you recycle cans or plastic, the materials are broken down and used again in another form. The **rock cycle** works in a similar way. In the rock cycle, any of the three kinds of **rock—igneous**, **metamorphic**, or **sedimentary**—can eventually become one of the others.

The rock cycle shows how one type of rock can be recycled into another type of rock.

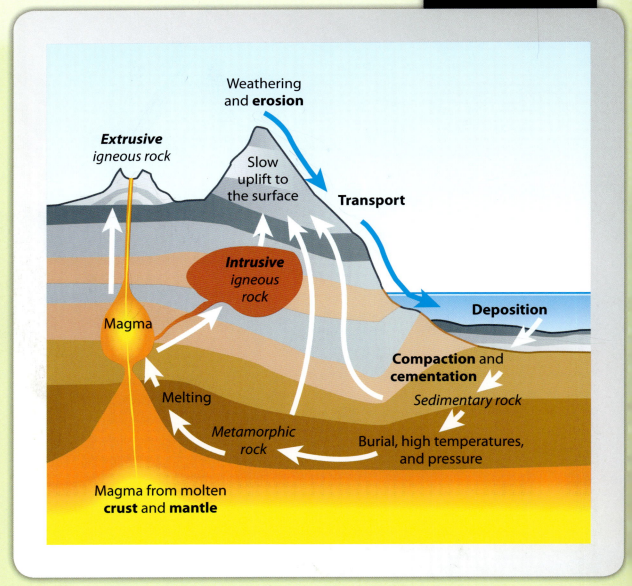

Look carefully at the diagram on page 6. Notice that there is no specific path that a rock takes through the cycle. Igneous rock at the surface can break down and reform as sedimentary rock. Igneous rock below the surface can be heated to the point that it changes and becomes metamorphic rock. Still other igneous rock beneath the surface can melt again and mix with a new pool of **magma**. When that magma hardens, a whole new form of igneous rock has formed. As you can see, metamorphic and sedimentary rock also forms, breaks down, moves, and forms again in several different ways.

Nothing new

Did you know that one of the **atoms** in the paper or the ink on this page might have been part of a dinosaur 500 million years ago? Or part of the ancient oceans three billion years ago? **Elements** on Earth are not destroyed, they do not disappear, and they do not leave the planet. And, other than the occasional meteorite entering from space, new materials do not come in either. The Earth has recycled the same atoms and elements that are here today for billions of years.

Elements on Earth constantly move through all different types of **matter**.

Minerals and Rocks

Steps to follow

1 Pour the hot water into the jar. It is important to keep the water warm throughout the process. Carefully warm it (about 15-30 seconds in the microwave) when you feel it get too cool.

2 Begin adding the salt one teaspoon at a time. Stir until the salt dissolves after each teaspoon you add. Stop adding salt when the last teaspoon you added will not dissolve.

3 Add a few drops of food coloring to the solution and stir.

4 Tie one end of the floss to the paper clip. Tie the other end around the middle of the pencil.

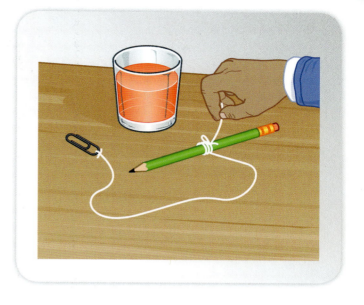

5 Rest the pencil across the mouth of the jar, with the paper clip dangling in the saltwater solution. The paper clip should hang down nearly to the bottom of the jar, but should not touch it.

6 Wait 24 hours, and look to see what is happening. Use a magnifying glass to get a close look at your results.

7 Let the experiment continue for several days, and see how your results change.

Minerals are everywhere

You have grown a crystal of the **mineral** halite, or rock salt. Salt is important to all people. Our bodies cannot function without it. Salt was important throughout history as a food preservative. It is used today to keep roads free of ice in places that have icy winters. Salt is also the raw material from which chlorine is made. Chlorine is a powerful disinfectant used to keep swimming pools and drinking water safe. Salt is just one of the many minerals that people use in their everyday lives.

Workers in Thailand harvest salt from a salt marsh.

Salt

Every time you turn on the lamp in your room, you use the minerals copper (in the wiring) and quartz (in the bulb). When you use a pencil, you're using graphite (in the lead), and when you use a quarter at the store, you are using nickel and copper. These are only a few examples of the many minerals that people use every day. But what exactly is a mineral?

All over the world, different peoples have harvested salt for thousands of years. In many places, methods of collecting salt have stayed much the same over this period. Because of its importance to human survival, salt has always been a valuable trade good.

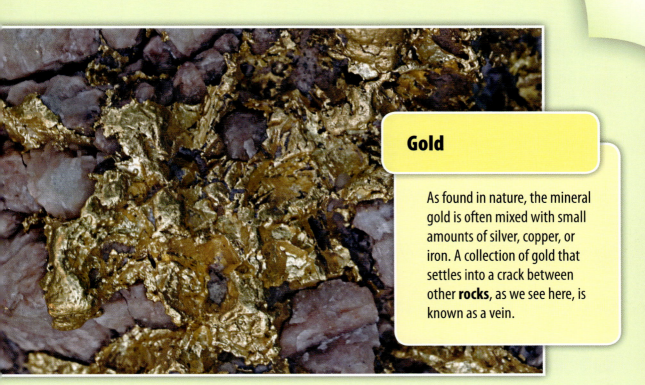

What is a mineral?

A mineral is a kind of **matter**. But what makes it different from other kinds of matter? A mineral must have the following characteristics:

* *It occurs naturally.* People cannot make a new mineral. Minerals can only form naturally.

* *It is a solid.* There are three main types, or states, of matter: solid, liquid, and gas. Minerals cannot be a liquid or a gas.

* *It has a definite chemical makeup.* This means that specific **elements** combine to make each different mineral. Scientists can test samples of minerals and identify them by the elements they find.

* *Its **atoms** are arranged in a certain pattern.* Inside a mineral, the atoms that combine are not mixed together in any old way. They are grouped together in a very definite pattern. This pattern is repeated over and over again, and all of these units, called crystals, are linked tightly together. This is what makes a solid so *solid*.

* *It was never alive.* A mineral cannot come from anything that is or once was alive.

Where are minerals and rocks in the Earth?

The Earth is made up of several layers. The center of the Earth is called the **core**. Closer to the surface is where rocks and minerals are found, in layers called the **mantle** and the **crust**. The mantle is a thick layer of very hot rock and minerals. The crust is a much thinner layer that includes the surface of Earth. The crust is where people actually come into contact with rocks and minerals.

Earth's inner core

Earth's center is divided into an inner and an outer core. The inner core is a solid ball made up of the elements iron and nickel. It measures 2,400 km (1,490 miles) across.

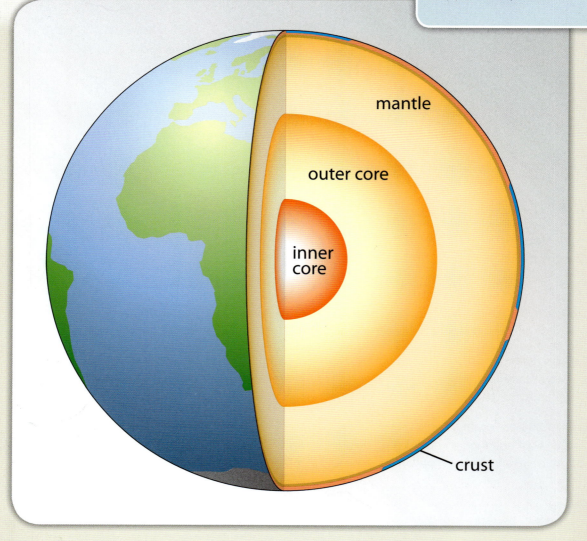

mantle

outer core

inner core

crust

How do people get minerals?

People remove useful minerals from the Earth by a process called **mining**. Several different mining methods are used because minerals are found in all kinds of situations. Surface mining is used to remove minerals that appear on the very outer layer of Earth's crust. Massive digging machines pull up large scoops of earth. Usually, this earth is not made up of useful minerals alone. But if there is enough of the useful mineral present, the earth is called an **ore**. For example, copper ore may only be about 1 percent copper. After the ore is dug from the ground, the copper is separated and sold to make wiring, pipes, household goods, and many other products that people want. The other 99 percent is discarded.

Surface mining sometimes causes nasty environmental problems. After the machines dig out the ore, a giant, ugly hole is left in the ground. The exposed rock walls can also interact with water to create dangerous acids. New techniques can lessen these problems, but old mining areas can remain damaged for many years.

Copper mining has badly scarred this landscape.

Igneous Rocks

Steps to follow

Melted "minerals"

For this activity you will need:
* Half a cup of chocolate chips
* Half a cup of butterscotch chips
* Half a cup of peanut butter chips
* A nonstick saucepan
* A greased bowl with at least a 1-pint (16-oz.) capacity.

1 Put all three kinds of chips into the saucepan.

2 Along with your adult helper, heat the chips over a low heat on the stovetop, stirring them every few minutes.

3 When they are completely melted, ask an adult to pour the mixture into the greased bowl. Allow the mixture to cool overnight.

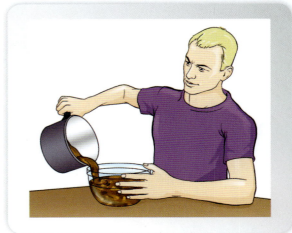

4 Remove the mixture from the bowl and set it on a towel so you can observe it. What do you see? Describe how the finished product is different from what you started with.

Note: Keep your "rock" for the next experiment.

⚠ **Warning**: Adult help will be needed for this experiment.

Melted rocks that are cool

The experiment on the previous page is a model of how **igneous rocks** are made. Each kind of chip was like a different **mineral**. The minerals that melt and mix to become actual igneous rocks are heated deep within the Earth, where temperatures can be as high as 1,250 °C (2,282 °F). The hottest temperature ever recorded at the surface of the Earth was only 58 °C (136 °F)!

Igneous rocks are classified by what minerals and **elements** are in them. For example, granite contains mostly silicon and aluminum. Another igneous rock, rhyolite, is also mostly silicon and aluminum. How are the two different? Igneous rocks are also classified by where they form. **Extrusive igneous rocks**, such as rhyolite, form when **lava** cools after reaching the Earth's surface. **Intrusive igneous rocks**, such as granite, form when **magma** cools within the Earth. (Pockets of magma within the Earth may take up to 1,000 years to cool!) Rhyolite and granite have different colors and patterns. They also have different textures, or they feel different.

Devil's Tower

Devil's Tower is in the U.S. state of Wyoming. Long ago, it was an intrusive igneous formation. Over time the **sedimentary rock** that surrounded it was worn away, and the tower was exposed.

Steps to follow

Igneous rock cycle

For this activity you will need:

* Your rock from the experiment on page 14
* A cup of white chocolate chips
* A nonstick saucepan
* A greased bowl with at least a 2-pint (32 fl. oz.) capacity.

1 Put your rock back into the saucepan and place the pan on the stovetop. Ask your adult helper to turn the heat to low.

2 Heat until the rock is completely melted again. Add your new "mineral," the cup of white chocolate chips, to the mix, stir them in well, heat them until they melt, and turn off the heat.

3 Pour the mixture into the greased bowl and let it cool over night.

4 Once it is cool, compare its appearance to that of the original rock.

 Warning: Adult help will be needed for this experiment.

From igneous to igneous

Can igneous rock turn into different igneous rock? Look back to the picture of the **rock cycle** on page 6. If you follow the different paths that **rock** can take in the rock cycle, you will see that igneous rock can return to deep within the Earth (where it had been magma to begin with) and melt again. Once it melts again, it is normal for the melted igneous rock to mix with new minerals. When this new mixture finally has a chance to cool and become igneous rock again, it will be a different kind of rock.

Some intrusive igneous rock that stays beneath the surface can simply be melted again by heat that flares up nearby. But how do extrusive igneous rocks get so deep down again that they can melt and become part of the rock cycle again? One important way is through a process known as **plate tectonics**.

Lava in Hawaii cools to become igneous rock.

What on Earth are plate tectonics?

It's hard to imagine, but the surface of the Earth is not a solid coating, like the peel on an orange. It is more like a giant, spherical jigsaw puzzle. In this case, the pieces are called tectonic plates, and they are slowly, constantly moving. The theory of plate tectonics describes the movement of these plates. The continents are part of these plates, so they are always on the move, too. The production of magma, lava, and igneous rock takes place where these plates push together or push apart. It is sometimes a destructive process, as you will see.

Earthquakes

In general, earthquakes happen when two tectonic plates slip past each other suddenly. The sudden release of energy causes the Earth to shake, often with a powerful force. Large, disastrous earthquakes often happen when tectonic plates come together.

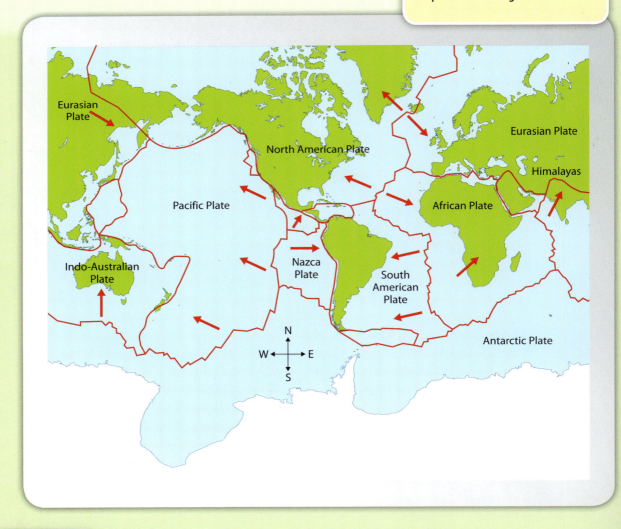

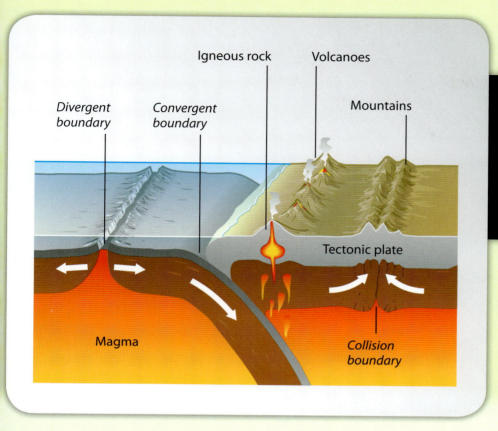

Igneous rock   Volcanoes

Mountains

Divergent boundary   *Convergent boundary*

Tectonic plate

Magma

Collision boundary

The places where plates meet

In many places where tectonic plates meet, the two plates diverge, or move away from each other. This is known as a **divergent boundary**. Magma is pushed up into the space between the plates, pushes the plates apart, and then cools. In this way, igneous rock is made as part of the rock cycle. When more magma pushes up, the process repeats, and the plates move a little farther apart.

In other meeting places, two plates converge, or move toward each other. This is called a **convergent boundary**. Sometimes one plate is forced beneath the other one. The rock that is part of the diving plate rubs against the plate above it, gets very hot, and begins to melt. This melted rock later rises through volcanoes and becomes new rock. This is another way that rock moves through the rock cycle.

Sometimes when two plates come together, neither plate goes beneath the other one. They collide. These **collision boundaries** make huge mountains. The Himalayas, the world's tallest mountains, formed when one plate moved into another one 65 million years ago!

Volcanoes

A volcano erupts when magma forces its way to the surface, creating a natural opening that is like a pipe or tube. But why does magma form—especially at a plate boundary where one plate goes beneath another one? When the plate goes under, it takes water with it. The presence of water makes it easier for rock to melt and become magma. The magma then rises because it is lighter than the solid material around it. Once it breaks the surface, the lava flows out, where it cools to become igneous rock.

Gases, ash, and rocks are also thrown out of an erupting volcano. For people, these can be the deadliest parts of a volcanic eruption. They can form a fast-moving cloud of super-hot ash and deadly gases that burns, chokes, and buries any living thing in its path. Volcanic gases and ash can also shoot high up into the air and change the weather by blocking out sunlight.

Rock and ash exploded into the sky when Mount St. Helens erupted in 1980.

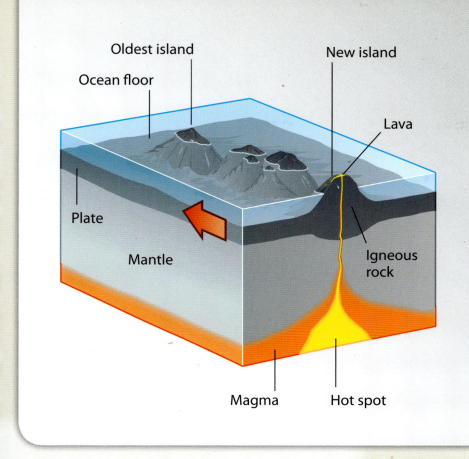

Oldest island

Ocean floor

New island

Lava

Plate

Mantle

Igneous
rock

Magma

Hot spot

As a tectonic plate passes over a hot spot, a chain of islands rises from the ocean.

Hot spots

Sometimes, volcanic islands, such as the Hawaiian Islands, just seem to appear in the middle of the ocean. Where do they come from? In these cases, hot magma from deep within the **mantle** is able to force its way through the middle of a plate. The place where magma rises up through the mantle is called a **hot spot**. The lava pours out onto the ocean floor, cools, and creates new igneous rock. Over time, the rock begins to pile up. After thousands of years, it is tall enough to break the ocean's surface, making a new island. During this time, the hot spot does not move. But the tectonic plate continues moving, slowly passing over the hot spot. So, a dotted line of islands tends to form.

The year without a summer

In 1815, Mount Tambora, a volcano in the Indian Ocean, erupted. The next year, 1816, was known as the "year without a summer" in eastern North America and northern Europe. Airborne ash from the eruption blocked sunlight, greatly lowering temperatures, ruining crops, and causing general misery. It snowed in June in Canada, and a cold rain fell for 142 out of 153 days between May and September in Ireland.

Metamorphic Rock

Steps to follow

1 Stack the three slices of bread in any order and squeeze them between your palm and cutting board so they only just stick together.

2 Cut the stack in half and observe the layers. This represents a **sedimentary rock**. Stack the two halves on top of each other, and wrap everything loosely in the wax paper.

3 Now use the rolling pin to really flatten out the stack. Unwrap it. How has its size changed? Cut it in half. How are the layers different? Does the "**rock**" feel the same?

Remarkable changes

The word "metamorphic" comes from "metamorphosis," which means "a change as if by magic." Maybe the flattened bread did not seem magical to you, but it is a simple way to model the processes deep within the Earth that we cannot copy. The **rock** that exists before it changes and becomes **metamorphic rock** is called the **parent rock**—in this case, the layers of bread in step 2. The pressure of the rolling pin smashing the bread brought about many of the same changes that metamorphic rocks go through. Metamorphic rock can have a different texture. It also may have a tightly banded appearance. Or, it may be much denser, meaning that more rock is packed into the same amount of space. Each one of these changes took place with the bread rock.

This is the metamorphic rock quartzite. It is a very hard rock, unlike its parent rock, sandstone, which is soft and flaky.

Change within a limited area

Sometimes the heat that changes a parent rock comes from a pocket of **magma** that builds up underground, but does not surface. (When it cools, this magma would become **intrusive igneous rock**. See page 15.) The heat of the magma heats the parent rock in the small area around it. In this limited area, where the heat is great enough, the particles in the parent rock can realign themselves, making a very different kind of rock. (See the **rock cycle** diagram on page 6. It shows that this parent rock can be **igneous rock**, sedimentary rock, or even metamorphic rock.)

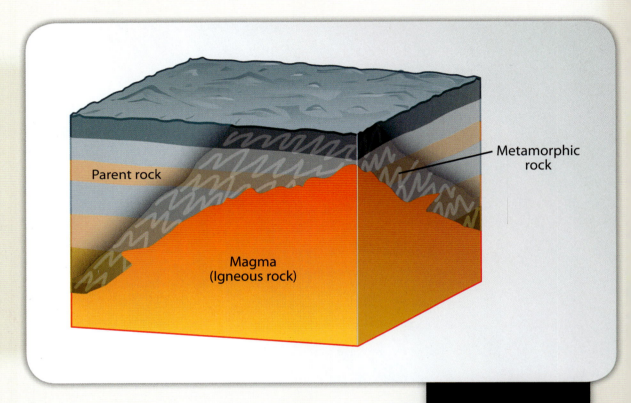

Parent rock

Metamorphic rock

Magma (Igneous rock)

Change over large areas

Dramatic conditions like the ones at a **collision boundary** often produce metamorphic rock over a large area. Parent rocks at this kind of boundary are bent, twisted, squeezed, and heated in the process of mountain building that happens there. All of these actions can cause rocks to undergo metamorphic changes.

Magma can push into layers of rock, heating those nearby until they become metamorphic rock.

Much of the
Taj Mahal in India
is made from
white marble.

People dig marble

Marble is a metamorphic rock. Marble's parent rock is generally limestone or another similar sedimentary rock. People throughout the ages have prized marble for a number of reasons. Most importantly, many people consider it to be beautiful. It is often pure white, but it comes in a variety of other colors and odd patterns, too. For example, black marble is found in parts of Poland, bluish-gray marble is found in part of Italy, and green marble is found in Pakistan. These colors show that other **minerals** were in the parent rock before metamorphism. Marble can be polished to a very glossy finish, which some people feel increases its beauty even more. Sculptors have used marble throughout the ages because they have found it to be easy to work with. It is fairly soft and rarely shatters when it is struck—perfect for hammering out a grand statue of a Roman general or a Greek god.

Sedimentary Rock

Steps to follow

1 Add the sand and both gravels to the bottle.

2 Fill the bottle about two-thirds full with water and put the cap on tightly.

3 Shake and swirl the contents around for about 15 seconds. Shake it up well!

4 Let the contents stand for a minute and look at the bottle from the side. Are the three different **sediments** mixed together or did they settle in layers?

Sorting sediments

For this activity you will need:

* A clear, empty 2-liter (half-gallon) soda bottle with a cap
* One cup of sand
* One cup of small gravel
* One cup of medium gravel (small enough to fit into the bottle's opening)
* Water.

Sediments eventually settle down

Sedimentary rocks form from smaller bits and pieces of other **rocks**. Mud, clay, sand, pebbles of different sizes—they're all small castoffs from much larger rocks. They can all be referred to as sediments. Sediments can come from **igneous**, **metamorphic**, or even sedimentary rocks.

The soda-bottle experiment showed how sediments mix and move in water. A sediment's size mostly decides how quickly it settles in water. In nature, rivers often move sediments of all sizes. When a river moving sediments enters a lake, the gravel tends to settle first, along with a little sand. The rest of the sand is carried a little farther, and the mud and clay go the farthest before settling. When this happens for a long time, thick layers of each kind of sediment build up. The layers at the bottom—with many, many layers over them—get squeezed. Sometimes this pressure, called **compaction**, is enough to turn sediments into rocks. Sometimes a cementing process makes it happen.

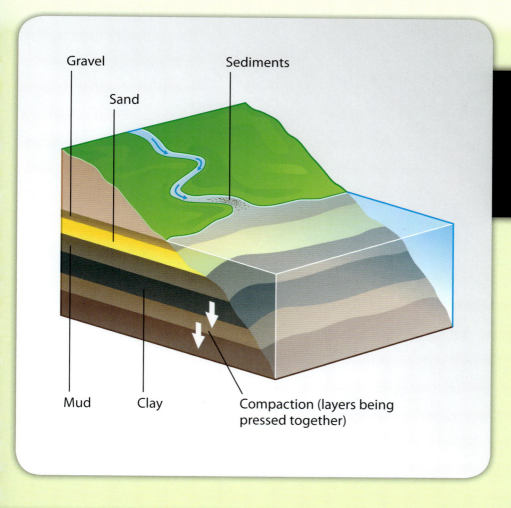

Gravel

Sediments

Sand

Mud

Clay

Compaction (layers being pressed together)

Compaction can press layers together to make sedimentary rock.

Steps to follow

1 Put the gravel in one of the paper cups. In the other cup, mix 235 ml (8 fl. oz.) of glue with 60 ml (2 fl. oz.) of water.

2 Pour about half of the glue/water mixture into the cup of gravel and mix everything around. Is all of the gravel well coated with the mixture? (This will vary depending on the size of the gravel you use.) If not, pour in as much as needed to coat the gravel.

3 Use your fingers to press the coated gravel solidly into the cup.

4 Let the mixture stand in a warm, dry place for 24 hours. Cut away the cup. What is your result?

Cementation

For this activity you will need:

* Two 355-ml (12 fl. oz.) paper cups
* 235 ml (8 oz.) of small gravel pieces
* A bottle of white glue (also called wood glue)
* Scissors
* Water.

Sediments stick together

When you cut away the cup, you should have a sedimentary rock. But you glued it together—isn't that cheating? Actually, this is similar to the way some sediments naturally bind together to form sedimentary rocks. **Minerals** in nature's waters act just like the glue in the experiment. As the sediments settle and compact, the water that holds the cement is squeezed out. The minerals are left behind, and they glue the sediments together. This process is known as **cementation**.

Sedimentary rock and art

Over thousands of years, sculptors have chosen to use many different sedimentary rocks in their works. An ancient Egyptian artist carved this figure of the goddess Taweret from the sedimentary rock called breccia. Notice that even in this statue's polished form, the many large gravel sediments are clearly visible. Between the large rock pieces are sands and the minerals that cemented the breccia together.

Sedimentary rock from minerals and water

Wherever there is a natural water source—a lake, the ocean, an underground pool—there are small amounts of minerals in it. Sometimes these minerals form unique kinds of sedimentary rock. For example, over millions of years of history, shallow saltwater seas spread out over flat lands and evaporated countless times. Every time a shallow sea evaporated, a layer of sediment—halite crystals—was left behind. Over time, thousands of layers built up, and the upper layers pressed down and compacted the lower layers into rock salt. Some deposits of rock salt can be 305 meters (1,000 feet) thick!

Rocks from things that were once living

Minerals cannot be made up of formerly living things, but rocks can. Coal is made up of the compacted remains of swamp plants that died millions of years ago. Layers and layers of sediments built up on top of the remains over time, compacting them into coal.

Fossilized fern leaves are often visible within pieces of coal.

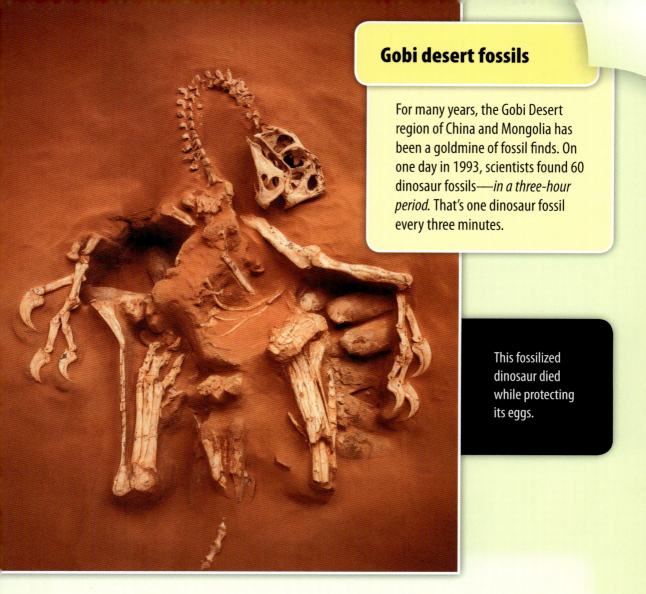

Gobi desert fossils

For many years, the Gobi Desert region of China and Mongolia has been a goldmine of fossil finds. On one day in 1993, scientists found 60 dinosaur fossils—*in a three-hour period.* That's one dinosaur fossil every three minutes.

This fossilized dinosaur died while protecting its eggs.

Fossils

Fossilized plants and animals show us what living things were like millions of years ago. Some of them seem quite bizarre to us. Did you ever wonder how they came to be fossilized? All fossils appear in sedimentary rock. Fossils can only form when they are buried under sediments. Most of them have to be buried quickly, before they decompose (rot) and leave no trace. Could fossils form in **igneous rock**? Well, **lava** sometimes buries things quickly. But lava would instantly burn any dead plant or animal, leaving nothing behind. What about **metamorphic rock**? Metamorphism happens deep within the Earth and at extreme temperatures and pressures. This process usually destroys any trace of fossils from sedimentary **parent rocks**.

Weathering

Steps to follow

Ice cold weathering

For this activity you will need:

* Two charcoal briquettes
* Two sealable plastic bags
* Water
* A freezer.

1 Soak one of the briquettes in water overnight. (You may have to weigh the charcoal down in the water—it tends to float.)

2 The next day, take the briquette out of the water, put it in a bag and seal the bag. Also seal the dry briquette in a bag.

3 Put both bags in the freezer overnight.

4 Compare the two briquettes the next day. What do you think happened?

Nature versus rocks

Weathering is how natural forces break apart **rocks**. Weathering is an important part of the **rock cycle**. It is one of the main processes that produce **sediments**, which later become **sedimentary rocks**. Freezing the waterlogged charcoal should have caused it to break apart to some degree. In nature, water gets into cracks in rocks. In cold weather, the water freezes and expands, or gets larger. The pressure from this is enough to chip or crack even the hardest rocks. This process, called **frost wedging**, is a kind of weathering known as **mechanical weathering**.

Root wedging is another form of mechanical weathering. In root wedging, plants begin to grow in a hole or a crack in a rock. As the roots advance, they are strong enough to widen cracks more, cause new ones, or even split rocks open.

A tree's roots slowly but surely work their way into solid rock.

Shell game

For this activity you will need:

* An egg
* White vinegar
* A bowl.

1 Put the egg in the bowl. The sides of the bowl should be at least 5 cm (2 in.) higher than the top of the egg.

2 Completely cover the egg with white vinegar.

3 Let it sit overnight. What do you see the next day? Reach in and gently touch the egg with your finger. What is different?

Chemical weathering

This experiment is a model of **chemical weathering**. The eggshell is made of a **compound** called calcium carbonate. The vinegar is an acid that breaks down the calcium carbonate. In nature, something similar happens. Rainwater can become naturally acidic and break down a variety of different rocks and **minerals**. Sometimes the rocks simply break apart. Other times they weaken in a certain place and a crack forms. This leaves the rock open to frost or root wedging.

Karst landscapes

Industrial pollution and car exhaust contribute to forming what is known as acid rain. Acid rain is much stronger and much more damaging to the environment than is naturally acidic rainwater. Acid rain greatly harms plant and animal life in forests. It also falls into streams and lakes and kills insects, fish, frogs, and other wildlife.

Karst landscapes are settings produced by chemical weathering. Naturally acidic rainwater acts on a sedimentary rock, such as limestone. Over time, lots of caves, shafts, and sinkholes develop. This photograph shows the Karst landscape in France.

Weathering and the rock cycle

Weathering is important to the rock cycle in several ways. Without weathering, parts of the cycle would not even be there. **Igneous rock** and **metamorphic rock** would only be able to melt or metamorphose. No other process could move them through the cycle. Sedimentary rock would not exist at all without weathering. Mechanical weathering slowly chips away at huge rocks of all kinds. But it also reduces small rocks to tiny rocks. Eventually this process produces the gravels, sands, clays, and muds that are compacted or cemented into sedimentary rock. Chemical weathering also breaks down many of the minerals that become limestone and other similar rocks.

Plastic sand

A recent study claimed that as much as one-quarter of the world's beach sand is now actually made up of tiny grains of plastic. They have now become part of the rock cycle, too.

Large plastic things, such as this bottle, break down over time into tiny grains.

Soils

Weathering plays a crucial role for living things, too. **Soil** is a direct result of weathering. Without soil, sunlight and water would be hard-pressed to grow anything on this planet. There would be no food for plant-eating animals and no plant-eaters for meat-eating animals. Plants give off oxygen as a natural part of the process that keeps them alive. Without growing plants, there would be almost no oxygen floating in our air.

Soil is mostly made up of weathered rock particles of all different sizes. There is also some water and air in soil. The final ingredient in soil is **organic matter**. The word organic means "involving living things." In soils the organic matter is the remains of things that were once living.

Soils differ all over the world. Different rocks make different soils when they weather and break down. Also, the number of plants, animals, and other living things that live, grow, and die in a given area makes a huge difference. The more organic matter in the soil, the more fertile it is. Fertile means "able to support plant life." Lastly, the amount of water in a soil is important to how fertile it is. The soil that supports a lush meadow holds much more moisture than barren desert soil.

Rich soil with lots of water and organic material helps all kinds of plants grow.

Erosion

Steps to follow

Soil on the move

For this activity you will need:

* A 23 cm x 33 cm x 5 cm (9 in. x 13 in. x 2 in.) cake pan
* Enough dirt to fill the pan
* A 23 cm x 33 cm (9 in. x 13 in.) section of sod (you should be able to buy this at a garden center)
* A watering can full of water (should be about two liters / half a gallon)
* Gardening gloves.

1 Wearing gardening gloves, fill the cake pan with the dirt. Pack it in fairly solidly, and level it off across the top.

2 Prop one end of the pan up about 15 cm (6 in.) and begin pouring the water from the can onto the raised end. What happens?

3 Clean out the pan and put the section of sod in the pan. Refill the watering can.

4 Prop the pan up about 15 cm (6 in.) on one end again and pour the water on the raised end in the exact same way. What happened this time?

 Warning: Adult help will be needed for this experiment.

Erosion moves weathered particles

Step 2 of the experiment showed what **erosion** is. The running water shifted the weathered particles that make up **soil**. Notice that very little soil eroded when living plants were present. (There is more on this on page 41.) Look back at the drawing of the sorting of soils on page 27. The movement of the river is what causes the **sediments** to travel downstream. The process of the sediments coming to rest after erosion is called **deposition**. An area where large amounts of sediments come to rest is called a deposit.

Although the water moves the sediments, it is the force of gravity that moves the water. Rivers flow the direction they do because that direction is downhill. Gravity also causes erosion on hillsides and mountainsides. Mudslides, landslides, and rockslides can send large amounts of material downward at frightening speeds. Heavy rains or earthquakes often trigger these events.

Heavy rains caused a mudslide that destroyed much of this village.

Wind also causes erosion

Winds act the same way that a river does. A strong wind, just like a fast-moving river, can pick up sediments of all sizes and move them some distance. Deposition sorts these sediments in the same way, as the wind drops heavier sediments earlier and lighter ones later.

This loess landscape was formed by erosion and has since been eroded even more, forming these hills.

Wind erosion has some interesting and unexpected results. Sand dunes form as a result of blowing winds. As the sand rolls and tumbles along a beach, it begins to pile up against a log, a **rock**, or even a sand ripple. If plants begin to take root, the growing dune can better hold onto its own sand, and more and more new sand piles up. The huge sand dune known as Big Daddy, in the African nation of Namibia, is one of the world's tallest. It is more than 305 meters (1,000 ft.) high! **Loess** soils are another result of wind erosion. Loess soils are formed when winds deposit very fine sediment particles in the same area over thousands, or even millions, of years. Some loess deposits in China are as deep as the Big Daddy dune is high.

Erosion can have harmful effects

Water and wind erosion can sometimes strip away valuable soils. Plants help to keep soils from being carried off. Look back to the experiment on page 38. What happened when you poured water on the sod? Did the soil wash away like the dirt that was in the pan by itself? The roots of the grass helped to keep the sod dirt in place. In nature, the same is true. Unfortunately, it is often the actions of humans that cause erosion. One method of logging, called clearcutting, removes all the trees in an area at one time. This is especially harmful on a hillside. With no tree roots to hold the soil, the next big rain can wash it all away.

The Dust Bowl

In part of the Midwestern United States in the 1930s, wind erosion created a disastrous situation. But it was human actions that were really to blame. Farmers replaced natural grasses with wheat and other crops. When poor rainfalls were unable to keep the crops growing, there were no more roots to hold the soil, and it began to blow away. Strong winds caused black blizzards that sometimes blocked out the sun. Dirt piled up like drifts of snow. Many farms failed, and people lost their land.

Nature: The Ultimate Recycler

The **rock cycle** is just one of many cycles that is constantly in motion on Earth. Another is the carbon cycle.

The carbon cycle

The **element** carbon is present in every living thing. It is in and around all of us. When animals and humans breathe, they give off the **compound** carbon dioxide. It becomes part of the air, where plants can put it to use. Plants use carbon dioxide, along with sunlight and water, to create energy for themselves. When plants and animals die and decompose, or rot, carbon again is released into the air.

The burning of oil, gas, and coal releases carbon into the atmosphere, too. We are only just beginning to see that nature cannot handle the amount of carbon that cars, factories, and power plants release into the air. During the next century, people must find a way to reduce their carbon output while giving nature a hand in recycling. If we do not there may be grave results for our planet.

The release of carbon from car exhaust pipes adds to the damaging process of global warming.

As you have learned, nature's cycles are powerful, and the rock cycle is especially so. While humans are able to tamper with and alter the carbon cycle, the rock cycle is much less vulnerable. In fact, for the most part, humans are at the mercy of the rock cycle. Is it possible to keep a volcano from erupting? Or keep a tectonic plate from sliding? If it were possible, we would have already done it. But would that be the right thing to do? Maybe using human ingenuity to better blend in with nature and its cycles would bring better results for the future of our planet.

The rock cycle often creates beautiful landforms, seen here in the White Cliffs of Dover, England.

Glossary

atom single particle of an element

cementation process by which dissolved minerals act as glue to stick sediments together and form sedimentary rock

chemical weathering process by which rock is broken down by being changed into another substance

collision boundary where two tectonic plates crash into each other and push up mountains

compaction process by which sediments are pressed together to form sedimentary rock

compound combination of two or more different elements that together make up a new substance. Water is a compound.

convergent boundary place where two tectonic plates are converging, or moving toward each other

core center of the Earth, which is made up of the inner core and the outer core

crust thin layer of rock above the mantle that includes the Earth's surface

deposition the coming to rest of eroded sediments

divergent boundary place where two tectonic plates are diverging, or moving apart from each other

element substance that cannot be broken down into simpler substances

erosion physical movement of weathered materials from one place to another

extrusive igneous rock type of igneous rock that forms when lava cools and hardens at the Earth's surface

frost wedging kind of mechanical weathering where water freezes in the crack of a rock and breaks the rock apart

hot spot place where magma forces its way through the middle of a tectonic plate

igneous rock rock that forms when molten rock cools and becomes solid

intrusive igneous rock type of igneous rock that forms when magma cools and hardens beneath the Earth's surface

lava liquid, molten rock that comes out of a volcano

loess soil formed when winds deposit very fine sediment particles in the same area over thousands, or even millions, of years

magma molten rock found deep within the Earth. Magma can reach the surface, and is then called lava.

mantle thick layer of very hot rock and minerals found between the outer core and Earth's crust

matter anything that exists as a solid, liquid, or gas

mechanical weathering process by which rock is physically broken down into smaller pieces

metamorphic rock rock that forms when old rocks are heated or compressed until they change into new, different rocks

mineral solid substance found in nature

mining process by which valuable minerals are removed from the Earth

ore rock that has a high enough percentage of a useful mineral to make mining worthwhile

organic matter substance made up of living or formerly living materials

parent rock rock which is heated or compressed to become a metamorphic rock

plate tectonics scientific theory that describes the movement of the plates that make up the surface of the Earth

rock group of minerals that is bound together to make a new substance

rock cycle continuous process in which rocks change, move, break down, come together, and become rocks again

sediment small bits of rock, minerals, or organic matter

sedimentary rock type of rock that forms when small bits of materials, called sediments, are compressed or cemented together, or when layers of broken up minerals build up

soil loose mixture made up of weathered rock, along with smaller amounts of organic matter, water, and air

Find Out More

Books

Spilsbury, Louise and Richard. *The Disappearing Mountain and Other Earth Mysteries.* (Chicago: Raintree, 2006)

Stille, Darlene R. *Plate Tectonics: Earth's Moving Crust.* (Minneapolis, Minn.: Compass Point Books, 2007)

Symes, R.F. *Rocks & Minerals.* (New York: DK Children, 2008)

Woods, Mary B and Michael Woods. *Volcanoes.* (Minneapolis, Minn.: Lerner Publications Company, 2007)

Websites

Earthquakes for Kids
www.earthquake.usgs.gov/learning/kids
This website has photos, puzzles and games, cool earthquake facts, and even a guide to the latest earthquakes all over the world.

Geology.com
www.geology.com
This website brings readers a constant flow of cutting-edge news on what's happening with **rocks**, **minerals**, and the Earth.

U.S. Geological Survey
www.usgs.gov
This science organization focuses on the study of biology, geography, geology, and water.

Places to visit

Devils Tower National Monument

P.O. Box 10
Devils Tower, WY 82714
Tel: (307) 467–5283

www.nps.gov/deto

Devils Tower National Monument was the first national monument in the United States, declared by President Theodore Roosevelt in 1906. The park offers a guided walk with a park ranger, and there is also a junior ranger program you can sign up for at the visitor center.

Grand Canyon National Park

P.O. Box 129
Grand Canyon, AZ 86023
Tel: (928) 638-7888

www.nps.gov/grca

The Grand Canyon is one of the most studied landscapes in the world. It offers a wide range of rock types, and is considered to be one of the finest examples of land **erosion** in the world.

Index